Gary Jones

Rome

Contents

Introduction   1

The Best Time To Visit Rome   3

Transport and Safety   6

History of Rome   19

Historical Sites   28

Coffee in Rome   47

Where to Eat and Drink   51

Nightlife   55

Hotels   58

3 Day Itinerary   61

Conclusion   65

1

Introduction

What do you think when you hear the word Rome? Does it make you think of the Papacy or Pope, The Vatican City, The Sistine Chapel or the Famous Saint Peter's Basilica?

Well, Rome is more than just that; these are just a drop in the vast world of what Rome is all about. Rome, also known as Roma in Latin, is the capital of Italy and the capital of the region of Lazio and the capital of the Province of Rome. Actually, Rome boasts of being the only city in the world that serves as a capital to two states i.e. The Vatican and the state of Italy; how cool is that!

Boasting of 3.8 million to 4.2 million people in the large Rome metropolitan area, the city prides itself as one of the top most visited cities in the whole of Europe and the 18th most visited city in the world. Rome is just not an ordinary city; people call it Roma Aeterna (The Eternal City) for a reason.

I wrote this guide to make you short stay in Rome an enjoyable experience that you will never forget. This book will help you experience the best Rome has to offer in a short time.

I hope you have a great time in Rome!
Safe Travels!

2

The Best Time To Visit Rome

The best times to visit Rome is April, May, and starting from Late September and October. If you visit in summer, the summer heat coupled with the crowds in the city will just be unbearable. Actually, it is best to avoid visiting Rome in August since almost all Italians seem to have a culture of going on holiday during this period so you will probably find most shops and popular destinations closed.

When you travel too late or early in the year, you also risk finding many attractions closed or opening for fewer hours. Also, as you will notice, airfares tend to be lower as the shoulder season starts in early autumn making this period the best to visit this spectacular city. During this period, the days will probably be warm and the nights are likely to be slightly cool while the tour groups and student mobs will probably have vacated the city.

Given the many things to see in Rome, you need at least three days to see most of the places otherwise trying to squeeze everything in a day or two will probably only leave you tired and wishing that you could go home. In any case, just like Rome wasn't built in a day, don't expect to see it in one day either!

After knowing when to visit Rome, the next thing that you are probably thinking about is transportation and safety within and around the city. Let me take you through all that in the next section.

3

Transport and Safety

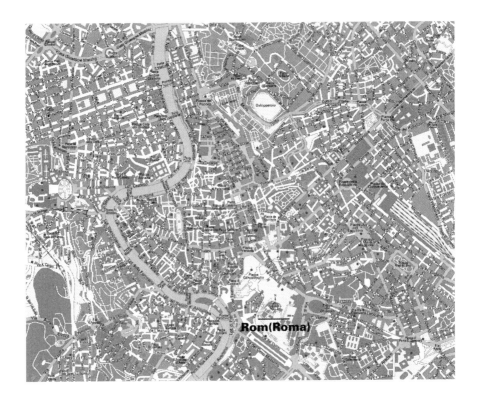

How to get into Rome
- **#1 By plane**

Rome has two main international airports:

1 Fiumicino/Leonardo da Vinci International Airport

This one is ultra modern and well connected to the city's public transport although the late night arrivals could probably limit you to only take an irregular bus or a taxi.

Airport Map
https://goo.gl/maps/BJch5D8WMdr
Phone:+39 06 65951

2 Ciampino/G.B Pastine International Airport

This one is located to the southeast of Rome. It is considered the low-cost airline airport serving Wizzair, Ryanair and Easyjet flights just to mention a few discount airlines in Europe. Although closer to the city center, the airport doesn't have a direct train connection. The airport is fairly small and closes overnight so you will probably be locked out of the airport until it opens again for the first checking at around 04.00 and 05.00. If you are flying into the city, it is best to sit on the right side of the plane since it will fly to the east of the city center so when the plane is reaching Rome, you can see the majestic Tiber river and the Olympic Stadium, St, Peters's, Castel Sant'Angelo and the Colosseum.

Airport Map
https://goo.gl/maps/XPsWem9MHKq
Phone:+39 06 65951

- **#2 By Ferry**

-You can use Grimaldi Lines that offer services from/to Tunis, Barcelona, Porto Vecchio(Corsica) and Toulon (France). However, these could be pretty much unreliable since they often run as much as 4 hours late, which means onward connections with train to Rome could be greatly disrupted. Also, the last ferry leaves Civitavecchia at midnight, which means that you could easily be stranded overnight.

-*You can also use Moby, which offers ferry services from/to Sardinia and Olbia.

Ferry Website
http://www.civitavecchiaport.org/
Phone:(+39) 3388117116
- **#3 By Car**

As the old saying goes, all roads lead to Rome so if you are traveling to Rome by road, you definitely won't be short of options. The city has a wonderful road connection called GRA or Grande Raccordo Anulare; any road that leads off GRA will get you to the city center but if you are going elsewhere, a good map or GPS will come in handy. The signs on the GRA usually show the name of the road that is leading to the center. For instance, it could be Via Aurelia, via Appia Nuova or via Tiburtina; you might probably not need these if this is your first time to be in Rome.

- **#4 By train**

The main railway station in Rome is known as Roma Termini; this is where most long distance trains pass through especially between 00.30 and 04.30 where they stop at Tiburtina railway station. There are also other railway stations like Roma Ostiense, Roma Tuscolana, Roma Tiburtina, and Roma Trastevere.

NOTE: Most long distance trains that are en route to other destinations will only stop for 1-2 minutes. Keep watch over your luggage wherever there are train stops since some thieves might try to grab them when the doors are closing.

Italia Rail Website
https://www.italiarail.com/
Email: info@italiarail.com

· **#5 By Boat**

If you are traveling on a cruise ship, it will probably dock at Civitavecchia. Some cruise ships will stay a full day to let passengers day trip to Rome while others will begin or end a cruise in Rome. So, what do you do if you arrive?

There will probably be many shuttle buses to and from the pedestrian port entrance where you might have to walk for about 10-15 minutes along the shore until you get to Civitavecchia train station. You will only incur a round trip train ticket of about €12 (as of 2014) allowing you unlimited access to tram, bus lines and Rome's Metro. There will be trains for commuters leaving almost every hour or even more frequently during rush hours. The journey could take about 80 minutes where you can choose to get off at Roma Trastevere train station or at Termini just right downtown whereby you will find trams, buses and Metro awaiting.

If you are starting or ending a cruise using a train, you will probably need to take a taxi between the ship and train station. Keep in mind that some platforms will only be reached through underground stairs/walkways so you have to know how you will get your luggage there; you could use the help of porters on site but ensure you keep watch.

If you are traveling on a modest-large sized yacht, it might dock at Porto di Roma at Ostia; this is a district that is located just 20KM from the city center and connected by Roma-Lido light railway. However, please note that the stations are not within a reasonable walking distance.

So, if you opted to travel by plane, you definitely need a way of moving from the airport to the city center (the same applies to if you want to travel to the airport).

Civitavecchia Website
http://www.civitavecchiaport.org/
Civitavecchia Extra Info Website
http://shorebee.com/en/italy/civitavecchia-rome/port
Email: info@shorebee.com

Porto di Roma Website
http://www.portoturisticodiroma.it/
Porto di Roma Map
https://goo.gl/maps/SVAxdmuiZZ72
Phone:+39 06 5618 8235

From the airport to the city center:
· **Travel by train, private or public bus**

From Fuimicino Airport
You can use either of the two train lines:

-*Leonardo Express
A train leaves the airport every 30 minutes to Roma Termini (this should be a 35 minute trip costing €14) platform #24. You can buy a ticket online within 7 days of departure. If you buy at the departure platform, you will have to pay €15. Please note that the ticket is for a route (Termini) and not for a specific train or time. Also, ensure that it is validated in a yellow validation machine before boarding the train. After validation, the ticket will expire within 90 minutes.

Suburban train (FL1 line)

-*Suburban train
This Train will not stop at Termini. Instead, you can get off at Tiburtina or at Ostiense station which is before Tiburtina after which you can connect to line B of the Metro. You can also get off at Roma Trastevere train station where you can then take a number 8 tram to head to Trastevere, Campo de Fiori and Piazza Venezia. This should cost you about €8 and €1.50 to cater for the tram metro ticket. You can as well get off at Tiburtina and Ostiense especially if are going somewhere close to the Metro station. As always, ensure your ticket is stamped in a yellow validation machine before you can use it.

-Terravision bus

This is the cheapest and easiest method of connecting between Fiumicino airport and the city center with a journey taking about 55 minutes and costing between €4-€6 for one way depending on whether you book online or at the station (round trip costs €11). You will trade your ticket with a "boarding pass" when boarding the coaches.

Schiaffini/COTRAL has buses on both airports. You can check the timetable here.

Bus Terravision Website
http://www.terravision.eu/airport_transfer/
bus-fiumicino-airport-rome/
Email:customerservices@terravision.eu
Cotral Website
http://www.cotralspa.it/

From Ciampino Airport

- -*The cheapest means of transport here is a combination of train and bus. First, take the bus (Atral/Schiaffini) to stop at Ciampino train station (5 minutes away) or at the Metro line A Anagnina Stop (10 or more minutes); either of these will cost about €1.20. Since Ciampino is the first or second train stop along the way to various destinations from Termini, you can just enter Ciampino in the automated ticket machines to give you different destinations or times. You can use a direct bus from Ciampino since these will take you to Termini station.
- -*You can use Sit Bus Shuttle that has a ticket costing €6 one-way or (€10 round-trip)
- -*COTRAL: This one has tickets costing €5 one-way
- -*Terravision: This has a bus that leaves the airport every 30 minutes costing €4 for one-way or €8 for round-trip

Sit Bus Shuttle Website

http://www.sitbusshuttle.com/en

Phone:(+39) 06.5916826

Bus Terravision Website

http://www.terravision.eu/airport_transfer/

bus-fiumicino-airport-rome/

- -*Taxis and Rental cars: The taxis in Rome are white costing a fixed rate of €48 from Fiumicino airport to downtown Rome. You can as well book a licensed limousine online for airport transfer.

Before you can even think of visiting the various spectacular destinations, the first thing you need to know is how the local transport system works; getting to or from the airport is just part of the entire thing. Here is how:

Travel within the city

First off, the historic Rome is not really large (about 1.5 miles or 2.5 km). Starting from Colosseum–Piazza di Spagna so you can move around on foot; many of the monuments are located within the same region. Nevertheless, if you want to move around you can opt to use different means of transport.

Metro

You can use the Roman Metro, which the residents fondly refer to as Metropolitana to travel round the historic city. It has 2 lines A (red) and B (blue). These two cross at the Termini Central station. You will find a train every 7–10 minutes starting from 5.30am–11.30pm daily; as for Saturdays, the train is available until 0.30am.

Metro Subway
http://goo.gl/LyaIHw

Tram

Six tram lines exist in Rome. You can use any based on where you are going.

Light rail
This will take you to parts of the city that are inaccessible through taxi or bus like Ostia Antica.

Segway
When you use this, you are considered a pedestrian, which means that you can navigate the streets much faster. Rental costs are about €25–50 per hour.

Segway Website
https://www.romebysegway.com/
Phone:(0039)0677591822

Electric buses
You can also use these to move around the city starting 5.30am until midnight.

Night buses

You will probably find over 20 night bus lines running from 0.30am-5.30am with the main stations being Termini (Piazza dei Cinquiecento) and Piazza Venezia. Normally, buses leave these two piazzas to all directions every 30 minutes with night bus stops being marked by an owl. Get more information here.

Bus Website
http://goo.gl/LyaIHw

Ho-Ho buses (hop-on/hop-off buses)

These are double-decker buses that have an open top with a ticket going for €18/20 on board the bus. The buses use different routes namely the Christian Rome and what is known as Archeobus that go to catacombs that is along the Appian way.

Bus Website
http://goo.gl/fc9skH

Rent a bike or a scooter

Traveling on 2 wheels will probably give you much more freedom on what to see. It will also make your movement around the city much faster making it a lot easier to see more. To rent one of these, it will cost you €40-€50 daily.

Rent Scooter Website
http://www.romarentscooter.it/
Rent Scooter Map
https://goo.gl/maps/q9g9rqohP5t
Address:Via del Paradiso, 42, 00193 Roma
Phone:+39 06 683 2222

Taxi

Only look for white or yellow taxis (metered). Also, always insist to have the taxi metered and have metered fare as opposed to an arranged price. The taxi driver could easily turn against you and demand for an unreasonably high amount of money.

Tip: Rome has public transport ticket inspectors who will fine you if they find you without a ticket on the trams and Metros. If you are found without a ticket, you might be forced to pay a fine of up to €50

Now comes the other important part, which is your safety. Let me explain how to stay safe when going to Rome.

Safety

Rome is safe even if you are a woman traveling alone; cases of violent crime are very minimal. Nevertheless, keep off places like Termini station especially at night as some rape cases have been reported in the past. Just as any other major tourist destination and city, pick pocketing is very high in Rome so keep a keen eye on your valuables. Rome was in 2010 ranked number 2 after Barcelona in cases of pick pocketing so watch out.

Also, don't tempt thieves by dangling valuable stuff like money, your camera and expensive jewelry. If you catch a pickpocket in the act, shout Aiuto, al ladro! (Help, Thief!). You can also report the matter to military police (in black uniform, and red stripped trousers) or the who pose as if they are trying to help; they are probably robbing you. So, as a rule of thumb, you can be a dick in Rome if you want to stay safe. In the hotel, leave your valuables with the hotel staff instead of the hotel safe.

Tip: Try to learn as much as you can about the strategies that pick pockets use in Rome to ensure that you don't end up a victim of pick pocketing.
Also, Rome has two rival teams in Serie A i.e. A.S. and S.S Lazio, which have strong rivalry that has at times been marked with rioting. To stay safe, don't wear anything that denotes that you support either team. Also, keep tabs on the football calendar in Rome to ensure that you don't end up being caught up in chaos. Other nearby teams that you don't want to wear their uniforms include Milan, Juventus, Inter Milan and Napoli. Only wear if you know what you are doing!

Tourist scams are also very popular in Rome so try to stay safe. Learn as much as you can on how these scams take shape at different times since the scam artists are always reinventing their strategies.

After knowing how to stay safe, the next part is visiting the magnificent buildings and other popular places to see what is left of them centuries after their construction.

18

4

History of Rome

With a history going as back as close to 3000 years, the city has seen most if not all human civilizations at their best and at their worst. A visit to the city will unravel the breathtaking Roman architectural masterpieces such as the massive Colosseum that date back thousands of years back, the finest works of Roman art that date back to Michelango's times, paintings and many other things that will make you bring back the BC moments in every step you take while touring the city.

That's not all; the modern Rome boasts of the finest restaurants serving Italian cuisine, bars and gelaterie coupled with a people that will amaze you with their humor, sense of style in their drinking and eating and many other aspects including soccer, films and fashion just to mention a few.

Rome has long been the capital of the Roman Empire making it to earn the name the city of the Roman Empire, Three Coins in the Fountain, La Dolce Vita (the sweet life), and the the Seven hills. For over millennia, Rome has served as a center of culture, religion and power throughout its close to 3000 years of existence making it to be named a UNESCO World Heritage Site that boasts of millennium old churches, Opulent monuments, grand romantic ruins like Pantheon, graceful fountains and ornate statues. Throughout its countless years in existence, Rome has seen rulers from different cultures in different times whose contributions to the growth or transformation of the city is evidenced by the different architectural masterpieces and works of art that you will find at different parts of the city.

Besides being a historic city, Rome prides itself as being one of the fashion capitals of the world with some of the oldest clothing and jewelry establishments having been found in Rome.

A Walk Down The History Lane Of Rome

Various legends try to explain how Rome was founded back in 735BC. Traditions explain that two mythical twins named Remus and Romulus who were the sons Mars and Rhea Silvia founded Rome on April 21 753 BC. Having been abandoned while they were infants, the twins were said to have been raised by a she-wolf (Lupa) long before Faustulus (a shepherd) found them and then raised them as his sons. Starting as a small village at the top of the Palatine Hill in the 8th Century BC, the city went on to become a center of the vast Roman empire that spun from Western Europe to Eastern Europe and also went on to become the center of the founding of Catholicism.

Since its foundation, it went on to become one of the oldest cities to be continuously occupied throughout Europe priding itself as having served as the capital of the Roman Kingdom, The Roman Empire and The Roman Republic. Actually, many refer to it as one of the important birthplaces of Western civilization. From the first century AD, the city has served as the seat of the Papacy, until 1870 when Rome became the capital of the Kingdom of Italy long after becoming the capital of the Papal States in the 8th century. In 1946, the city became the capital of the Italian Republic. Well, this only describes the political aspect of Rome, which is hardly representative of what exactly was taking place throughout the many years that the city has been in existence. We will move back in time to the middle ages.

As I already mentioned, Rome has served as the Papal seat for most of its years in existence putting it at a strategic position where it could grow tremendously. Almost all the popes who served in the Middle Ages starting from Nicholas V (1422–1455) put lots of effort in transforming Rome from what it was architecturally, artistically and culturally. Close to 400 years of architectural and urbanistic program was put forth to make Rome a big player during the Italian Renaissance. All that was made possible courtesy of some of the famous artists and architects of the time including Raphael, Michelangelo who created the sculpture of Moses, Bernini and Bramante who created masterpieces such as Raphael Rooms, Sistine Chapel, St Peter's Square and St Peters Basilica.

The ideal position of Rome at a ford on the Tiber River is what largely contributed to Rome becoming a center of trade and traffic since its formation. The city even grew much faster when it became the Roman Kingdom capital that was followed by a series of Etruscan Kings before it later became the capital of the Roman Republic in 509BC and later the capital of the Roman Empire between 27BC-285AD. From this period, Rome enjoyed the position of being the wealthiest, largest and the most powerful city all over Western Europe and the Mediterranean Sea even after the fall of the Western Roman Empire in 476AD.

Starting from Constantine I rule (306-337) the Pope, formerly known as the Bishop of Rome, the city grew in its political and religious importance transforming the city to become the center of the Catholic Church. Everything wasn't a smooth ride for the city and its residents. After the Western Roman Empire fell in 476AD, what followed was attempted sieges by Ostrogoths in 537 AD, and Saracan in 846 AD, all of which failed. However, this didn't last too long as the city was captured by the Normans in 1084AD.

The Middle Ages saw a decline in the city's population as the city was taking a new position as a capital of the Papal States that had been formed recently. The Middle Ages also saw most of the city's ancient monuments abandoned and ripped off. Most of these items were recycled in other constructions or baked to make new mortar to make new buildings.

Rome was also a center of struggles between the Roman nobles especially between the Papacy and the Holy Roman Empire and in 1309, the then Pope left Rome for Avignon at the request of the then King of France after which the city went into full chaos. When he returned in 1377, Rome changed a lot. This period saw the construction of extravagant churches, public places, bridges, Sistine Chapel, St Peter's Basilica etc to make Rome to equal the grandeur that other Italian cities of the time had.

In the next 200 years, most of the city's magnificent buildings were setup according to the Baroque architecture featuring famous artists like Bermini, Michelangelo and Caravaggio. The mighty St Peter's Basilica was constructed for over 100 years between 1506 and 1626. The Pontiff was later on forced to flee in 1798 when local revolutionaries rose against the Papal authority and declared a Roman Republic although this only lasted a year as the troops from the Kingdom of Naples conquered the newly found Roman Republic of the revolutionary movement.

The Napoleonic Troops occupied the city between 1805 and 1814. The locals also rose against the Papal government in 1849 and forced the Pontiff to flee the city to Gaeta after which a new Roman Republic was founded with a modern democratic constitution. With the aid of Napoleon III, the then French Emperor, the revolutionary forces were crushed at the last battle of Janiculum hill including the Goffredo Mameli, the composer of the Italian anthem.

The city also faced power struggle in 1860 following the rise of the Kingdom of Sardinia Piedmont who wanted to unite the peninsula. In the end, the Papal States were stripped off everything they had except Rome, which was under the French protection. This didn't last long though as the French troops abandoned it during the French-Prussian War making the city vulnerable and soon after, the city was captured by the newly formed Kingdom of Italy on September 20 1870. From this day to date, the city has remained the capital of Italy.

The newly formed Italian government started making new districts like Esquilino, monuments like Vittoriano and constructed various public buildings while tearing down many Medieval and Renaissance buildings to create a new street layout. Additionally, the Tiber River was also enclosed with the embankments that are still there today.

After the World War I and with the rise of Fascism in 1922, Rome saw drastic changes including creation of new districts like EUR and avenues like via dei Fori Imperiali and Via Dela Conciliazione. New public buildings were also constructed while stripping off the city of its ancient sites like the Circus Maximus and the Fora, which were excavated; this period simply saw neighborhoods that date back into the Medieval ages wiped out. This stopped when the Monarchy fell and the Italian Republic was formed in 1946.

As you can see, the modern Rome is what was left of the ancient times, Middle Ages and Renaissance blended with a twist of modernity to create one of the most beautiful cities on the planet boasting of millions of tourists every year. In addition, just like the old saying goes, Rome was not built in one day; its growth cuts through close to 30 centuries. So, how were the structures really built?

How The Structures Of The City Were Built

As I already said, Rome wasn't built in a day. The Romans started using concrete over 2000 years ago. Well, the concrete they used was much more than the concrete we use today; they had a fairly different formula that was not really as strong as the concrete we use today although the structures that they made like the Colosseum and Patheon have stood the test of times for centuries with little to no maintenance.

The concrete of the time was about 10 times weaker than the modern concrete but with exceptional resistance against various elements thanks to the use of volcanic ash. The formula for the concrete they made at the time was a perfect mix of limestone, which was burned to make quicklime after which water was added to make a paste after which the volcanic ash was added (three parts of volcanic ash was added to one part of lime). This volcanic ash reacted with the lime paste making a highly durable mortar, which was then combined with chunks of bricks the size of a fist or tuff (volcanic rocks) after which the mixture was packed to form walls, vaults and other structures. This is contrary to the modern concrete, which only contains cement, aggregates like fine gravel and sand.The ancient structures were the only ones built using this ancient formula; in the Middle Ages, the Romans seemed use a different formula for building their structures.

So, now that you know a general history of how the city came into being, I will take you through a short trip round the city so that you can get to know the history of the structures, when to visit, how much you will pay if you have to and other crucial details. Before we start off, you first need to understand when the best time is to plan your trip.

5

Historical Sites

The Colosseum (Flavian Amphitheater)

This was the largest building at its time and Emperor Vespasian, the founder of the Flavian Dynasty, started its construction in 72AD until its completion in 80AD just a year after Vespasian died. Even if the magnificent structure had some point fallen into ruins, it is still extremely beautiful.

The current name of Colosseum was because of the giant statue of Nero (Colossus) that is nearby. The elliptical structure measures 188m by 156m and a height of over 48 meters (159feet). It features 160 statues and is clad in marble. At its construction, the structure could accommodate up to 55000 spectators who could enter the building through over 80 entrances to watch the famous gladiators fight; you will see the remains of the arena when you visit the Colosseum. It features four stories with the upper story being made for women and lower classes.

An earthquake that struck in 847AD damaged the southern end of the Colosseum. The marble and the other materials were later on used to make other buildings like St Peters Basilica and Palazzo Farnese.

The Colosseum Map
https://goo.gl/maps/qb47NiTKubC2
Address:Piazza del Colosseo, 1
Phone:+39 06 3996 7700

Vatican City (Holy See)

This is the world's smallest country occupying around 109 acres or 44ha (0.17 sq mi (0.44 km2) with about 800 residents who are not permanent (comprises nuns, priests, guards, pope etc). It serves as the spiritual center for all Roman Catholics all over the world. When you visit the Vatican City, you will also see St. Peter's Basilica, Sistine Chapel and Vatican Museums. You should also expect to see some Swiss guards. You can learn more about the history of the Vatican here. When you visit the Vatican, it is best to have a tour guide to ensure that you don't miss anything important.

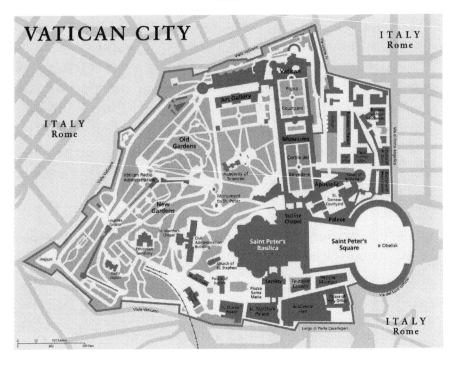

Vatican City Map
https://goo.gl/maps/yGoDZdGooBT2

Victor Emmanuel Monument

Officially, the monument is referred to as Monumento Nazionale a Vittorio Emanuele II. It was constructed as tribute to, Victor Emmanuel who became the first king of the new United Italy. The construction work started in 1885 with the first design being made by Guiseppe Sacconi although he died in 1905 before the structure can be completed.

Standing at 80m high and up to 120m wide, this magnificent structure has large stairs that lead to a huge colonnade. You will also see two fountains i.e. with the right one representing the Tyrrhenian Sea and the left one representing the Adriatic Sea. The center of the fountain has a statue of the Father of the Nation, Victor Emmanuel weighing up to 50 tons.

Victor Emmanuel Monument Map
https://goo.gl/maps/RpAh9HVRnnr
Address:Piazza Venezia
Phone:+39 06 678 0664

Vatican Museums

These were founded during the reigns of two popes, Clement XIV (1769-1774 and Pius VI (1775-1799) although the collection work started much earlier in 1480 when Apollo of Belvedere was founded (you will see that when you visit the museum). These museums have very many elegant stuff that have a long history so it is always best not to put too much pressure on yourself that you want to see everything in one visit; keep in mind that the museums stretch a distance of up to 7km (4.4 miles).

The museums you can expect to find along the way include Sistine Chapel, the Raphael Rooms, Beato Angelico, Loggia and the Borgia Apartment each of which have a long history and are filled with masterpieces of sculpture, painting and art work collected by various popes through centuries. Other notable museums include Gregorian Etruscan Museum, Gregorian Egyptian Museum, Vatican

Picture Gallery, Gregorian Museum of Pagan Antiquities, Chiaramonti Museum & the New Wing, Pio-Clementine Museum, Museums of the Vatican Library, Vatican Historical Museum and many others.

Vatican Museums Website
http://goo.gl/zAwaCB
Vatican Museums Map
https://goo.gl/maps/kqTGxhb3bEn
Address:Viale Vaticano, 00165 Roma
Phone:+39 06 6988 3332

Sistine Chapel

A visit to Rome wouldn't be complete without a visit to the Sistine Chapel. This is the official residence of the pope. Giovannino de' Dolci built the chapel in 1473-1481; this was originally meant to be a private chapel for pope, Sixtus IV. The interior painting is just a masterpiece created by Michelangelo.

Sistine Chapel Map
https://goo.gl/maps/sbkYvFr3LUF2
Address:Vatican City
Phone:+39 06 0608

St. John Lateran

This is where the pope currently officiates as the bishop of Rome. It was first constructed in 314AD although later damaged by an earthquake. Reconstruction work dates back in 1646–1666.

St. John Lateran Map
https://goo.gl/maps/cXcy7atDwMB2
Address:Piazza di San Giovanni in Laterano, 4

Phone:+39 06 6988 6433

Baths of Caracalla

Also known as The Thermae Antoninianae, it dates back in 217AD in the reign of Emperor Caracalla. It was once the biggest bath complex in the world and the baths were very functional for over 300 years.

Baths of Caracalla Map
https://goo.gl/maps/ZADGr8je8x32
Address:Viale delle Terme di Caracalla, Roma
Phone:+39 06 3996 7700

Forum of Trajan

This dates back to 106-113AD and was the last and the greatest imperial forums.Emperor Trajan gave the order to build this monument with the spoils of war.

Forum of Trajan Map

https://goo.gl/maps/MbWxuyPrS4v
Address:Via dei Fori Imperiali, 00186 Roma
Phone:+39 06 0608

Arch of Titus

This was built between 81 and 85AD to mark the capture of Jerusalem from Jewish Zealots.

Arch of Titus Map
https://goo.gl/maps/MWRrFxyXM912
Address:Via Sacra, 00186 Roma
Phone:+39 06 0608

Trajan's Column

This was built in honor of Emperor Trajan in 113AD.
Trajan's Column Map
https://goo.gl/maps/LemiS22FcYM2
Address:Via dei Fori Imperiali, Roma
Phone:+39 06 0608

Arch of Constantine

You should see this next to the Colosseum; it is the largest remaining Roman triumpha arches built in 315AD when Constantine defeated Maxentius in the battle of Milvian Bridge.

Arch of Constantine Map
https://goo.gl/maps/C6Tszx78xJu
Address:Via di San Gregorio, Roma
Phone:+39 06 0608

St Peters Basilica

This is the largest Roman Catholic church in the world and features Michelangelo's dome. It was constructed on Vatican Hill, which is just across river Tiber, the place where St Peter (the Bible apostle) died and was buried in 64AD; St. Peter is usually considered to be the first pope.

The construction of the basilica started when the first Christian emperor of Rome, Emperor Constantine decided to construct a basilica on the Vatican Hill where a small shrine marking the tomb of St. Peter had been marked; this took place in the fourth century.

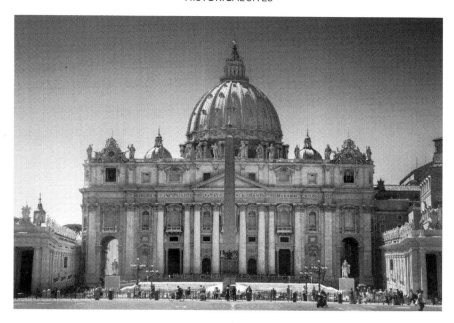

The construction work commenced in 319–322, the consecration took place in 326AD and the construction work was completed in 349AD. The Basilica was falling apart in the 15th century when the then pope Nicolas V ordered its restoration and enlargement after Bernardo Rossellino made plans. However, all work halted when Nicolas V died; no work was done for close to half a century until the then pope Julius II ordered the completion of the new basilica under Donato Bramante as the chief architect. Julius II laid the first stone in 1506 to what was to become the largest church in the world.

Michelangelo Buonarroti became the architect in 1547 after the death of Bramante in 1514 and after several architects made other changes to the design; he also included other changes including the dome. He (Michelangelo) died in 1564 when the drum of the dome was built; Giacomo Della Porta completed the entire construction in 1590. The construction took place in 1626 under pope Urban VIII, 1300 years since the first concentration took place.

There is a lot to say about this spectacular masterpiece that cuts across over 20 centuries; the floor, the paintings, tomb, narthex, front façade, apse and everything else in the basilica are just perfect. As you visit St. Peters Basilica, you will probably pass through St. Peters Square that has a history dating from the 17th century.

St Peters Basilica Website
http://goo.gl/j7nqH1
St Peters Basilica Map
https://goo.gl/maps/zYG4UbDLsUq
Address:Piazza San Pietro, 00120 Città del Vaticano, Vatican City
Phone:+39 06 6988 3731

Pantheon

Pantheon was built over 1800 years ago to serve as a temple of the gods. A look at this magnificent structure will bring back the Roman Empire. This building is more than 43m high and by 1436, it was one of the largest in the world until Florence Cathedral was built. The top of the dome has a large opening known as the oculus.

Pantheon Map
https://goo.gl/maps/vLztoscnj8N2
Address:Piazza della Rotonda, 00186 Roma
Phone:+39 06 6830 0230

Circus Maximus

This was once the largest stadium in the ancient Rome hosting up to 250,000 people, which was a quarter of the entire population in Rome. It hosted countless chariot races for close to a millennium. The track lies between Aventine Hills and the Palatine with the first permanent gates being made in 329BC. It was first built in the sixth century BC. The last known race was held on 549 AD.

Circus Maximus Map

https://goo.gl/maps/E151U3L0LE62
Address:Via del Circo Massimo, 00186 Roma
Phone:+39 06 0608

Trevi Fountain/Fontana di Trevi

This is probably the most famous and the very beautiful fountain in Rome. This magnificent fountain is located at the very end of the Aqua Virgo, a 19 BC aqueduct constructed by Agrippa, who was the son in law of Emperor Augustus. This aqueduct brings water from Salone springs, which is 21 km away and is responsible for supplying Rome's fountains with water.

A small sized fountain was first built in the 15th century after which it was expanded in 1732. The modern fountain measures 20m wide by 26m high with a width of about half the square. At the center is a figure of god of the sea (Neptune) riding a shell shaped chariot pulled by sea horses; everything here is just magnificent. You have to see for yourself!

Trevi Fountain/Fontana di Trevi Map
https://goo.gl/maps/KojPow6Ffcz
Address:Piazza di Trevi, 00187 Roma
Phone:+39 06 0608

Piazza Navona

This square has over 3 beautiful fountains nearing Baroque church of Sant'Agnese in Agone. Emperor Domitian built this structure in 86AD on former Stadium of Domitian. At its time, the stadium (also known as Circus Agonalis-competition arena) was much larger than the Colosseum; it was used for sporting activities and festivals. The stadium was however demolished to pave way for the Navona square in the 15th century although some of the remains of the Dimitian's stadium can still be seen around the area.

You can go on a guided tour to the underground monument starting from Piazza Tor Sanguigna 13. Here is what to see in Piazza Navona:

#1 Fountain of Four Rivers (Fontana dei Quattro Fiumi)

These are the biggest and the central fountains located at the Piazza Navona. Pope Innocent X constructed it between 1647-1651 with the design being first commissioned to Borromini, which was later on handed to Bernini. It features four figures that represent Rivers Nile, Ganges, Rio de la Plata and Danube. You can get more details here.

#2 Neptune Fountain and Moor Fountain

Also called Fontana del Nettuno, Neptune Fountain is located in the Northern while the Moor Fountain also called Fontana del Moro is at the southern end. You can learn more about these here and here.

#3 Church of Sant'Agnese in Agone

This was commissioned in 1652 by the then pope Innocent X with the construction work being done according to the legend St Agnes. The church was completed in 1670.

Piazza Navona Map
https://goo.gl/maps/VkgsbWzbc952
Piazza Navona, 00186 Roma

Others places worth mentioning include:
· **Villa Borghese**

This dates back in the 17th century.

Villa Borghese Map
https://goo.gl/maps/ncDK9P5GRST2
Phone:+39 06 0608

· **Castel Sant'Angelo**

This was built in 123AD.

Castel Sant'Angelo Map
https://goo.gl/maps/JNwExWqDqDu
Phone:+39 06 0608

· **Piazza del Popolo**

This features a 3300 year old obelisk taken from Egypt's Sun Temple.

Piazza del Popolo Map

https://goo.gl/maps/d6iWdDMJvo52
Phone:+39 06 0608
- **Mouth of Truth**

This was some sort of lie detector, whose mouth would close if someone put their hand in and told a lie. It is definitely worth checking out.

Mouth of Truth Map
https://goo.gl/maps/fDdBo5dSMQL2
Phone:+39 06 0608
- **Arch of Septimius Severus**

This triumphant arch was constructed in 203AD following victory of Emperor Severus.

Arch of Septimius Severus Map
https://goo.gl/maps/hzJfgetDPtv
Phone:+39 06 0608
- **The Theater of Marcellus**

Originally conceived by Julius Caesar, this was built by Augustus in 13BC. At its time, it was the largest and could occupy over 12000 spectators.

The Theater of Marcellus Map
https://goo.gl/maps/NYz1iNq1AGn
Phone:+39 06 0608

6

Coffee in Rome

Rome is one of the great cities of the world and is famous for many things, one of them is coffee.You have to drink a quality cup of coffee in Rome and enjoy one of the great cafe's and experience the Rome coffee culture.Let's take a look at some of the best coffee shops in Rome:

- ## Caffè Sant'Eustachio

Caffè Sant'Eustachio is one of the most historic coffee shops in Rome.Locals love to pop into this cafe and enjoy a quality cup of coffee.This coffee shop was founded in 1938, and the interior has stayed almost the same as back in the old days.This coffee house serves high-quality coffee that is mostly organic and fair trade coffee beans.If you get a table, it will be slightly more expensive than standing or taking your coffee out of the cafe. Caffè Sant'Eustachio is a classic Rome Cafe.

Address:Piazza di S. Eustachio, 82, Roma
Phone:+39 06 6880 2048
Caffè Sant'Eustachio Website
http://www.santeustachioilcaffe.it/en/
Caffè Sant'Eustachio Map
https://goo.gl/maps/QsLX8FpUmTN2

- ## Antigua Tazza D'Oro Coffee House

One of the best things about this cafe is that it is located right in front of the Pantheon, so if you want to grab a coffee after visiting the Pantheon, then this is the perfect spot.This cafe has a great homely atmosphere and serves great coffee.

Address:Via degli Orfani, 84, 00186 Roma
Phone:+39 06 678 9792
Antigua Tazza D'Oro Website
http://www.tazzadorocoffeeshop.com/
Antigua Tazza D'Oro Map
https://goo.gl/maps/1XfQLxRhTs42

- ## Ciampini

Ciampini is a very cosy cafe that has been run by the same family for four generations.This cafe serves excellent coffee and is famous for its warm and cosy atmosphere.If you are visiting Rome in the summer, then get a table outside.If you feel like you want to relax and rest after a long day in Rome, then this is a great place to regroup before going on your next adventure in Rome.

Address:Piazza di S. Lorenzo in Lucina, 29, 00186 Roma
Phone:+39 06 687 6606
Ciampini Website
https://www.facebook.com/barciampini
Ciampini Map
https://goo.gl/maps/PzCXTeUvQ2F2
· **Domiziano**

Domiziano has an amazing location and is located in front of Bernini's majestic Four Rivers Fountain.The coffee at this cafe has a unique twist and some of the coffee served has some alcohol in it.If you want to try out something different at a great location, then come to Domiziano for lunch and a cup of coffee with a twist.

Address:Piazza Navona, 88, 00186 Roma
Phone:+39 06 6880 6845
Domiziano Website
http://www.domiziano.it/en/index.php
Domiziano Map
https://goo.gl/maps/J3GmYekAtLs
· **Antico Caffè Greco**

Drinking coffee at Antico Caffè Greco is like going back in time.This cafe had an amazing history and opened in 1760.Great artists and thinkers like Casanova and Wagner use to visit this famous building in Rome.The building houses a large private gallery that is open to the public.Great spot for coffee and art.

Address:Via dei Condotti, 86, 00187 Roma
Phone:+39 06 679 1700
Antico Caffè Greco Website
http://www.anticocaffegreco.eu/
Antico Caffè Greco Map
https://goo.gl/maps/JEUTLNEQPz22

7

Where to Eat and Drink

When you go to Rome, act like Romans. Here are some tips on where to eat. There are countless places you can eat; but ensure that you don't fall prey of the tourist trap that restaurants sometimes have.

Tip: The best restaurants are outside the historical center; this is where Italians live and eat! Here are some things to ask for if you want to eat and dine like a Roman during your visit to Rome:

Panino: This simply means stuffed sandwich.

Cornneto & Cappuccino: This simply means croissant and cappuccino or coffee and creamy milk.

Carciofi alla giudia: Means Jewish style Artichokes (fried).

Carciofi alla romana: Means Artichokes in Roman Style.

Fiori di Zucca: Means Zucchini flowers that are prepared in deep fried batter.

Pizza al taglio: means pizza by slice.

Coda alla vaccinara: This refers to Oxtail stew.

Abbacchio "alla scottadito: This simply refers to lamb chops.

This list isn't conclusive. You can simply order whatever you find the restaurant serving! When you are in Rome, you are a Roman, remember! Nevertheless, since you may not have all the time to be going for lunch outside the historic center, you might still need to settle for nearby restaurants to save on time. Here are a few restaurants in and out of the historic center.

· **Flavio al Velavevodett**

Flavio al Velavevodett features seasonal Roman classics. You will get delicious foods such as deep fried shredded beef and polpette di bullito. Other common foods include artichokes, lamb, pasta dishes like cacao e pepe, carbonara etc. Here are the contacts to the restaurant.

Address: Via di Monte Testaccio, 97
Telephone +39 06 574 4194
Website
http://www.ristorantevelavevodetto.it/en/home
Flavio al Velavevodett Map
https://goo.gl/maps/woYtm54UVWK2

· I Vicini Bistrot

This has excellent food and perfect customer service. It is near piazza Navona and Panteon making it great for a lunch or dinner stop over after a busy day.

Address: Via di Monterone, 18, 00186 Roma
Telephone: +39 3668782625
Website
https://goo.gl/HzGD7R
I Vicini Bistrot Map
https://goo.gl/maps/S4ZfJ4wUpq92

· Likeat

This one is wonderful for Italian cuisines, sandwiches, fast food etc. You can visit here for breakfast/brunch, lunch, takeout and late night. It is also fairly affordable.

Address: Corso Vittorio Emanuele II 310, 00186 Rome, Italy
Telephone: +39 349 706 1072
Website
http://www.likeatroma.com/
Likeat Map
https://goo.gl/maps/N5BzPmamxAt

· Waraku

If you want to taste Japanese cuisine in Rome, this is the place to go. You can also make reservations.

Address: Via Guglielmo Albimonte 12–12A, Rome, Italy
Telephone: +39 329 724 8911
Waraku Map
https://goo.gl/maps/yJ11Qrf7th42

- **Pinsere Roma**

This is popular for serving authentic Italian Pizza and pasta.

Address: Via Flavia, 98, 00187 Rome, Italy
Telephone: +39 06 4202 0924
Website
http://www.pinsereroma.com/
Pinsere Roma Map
https://goo.gl/maps/cSCvsPc4TV62
- **Panino Divino**

The restaurant is widely known for serving breakfast/brunch, reservations and delivery. It has a wine bar, sandwiches etc at an affordable price.

Address: Via Dei Gracchi 11/a, 00192 Rome, Italy
Telephone: +39 06 3973 7803
Website
http://www.paninodivino.it/
Panino Divino Map
https://goo.gl/maps/xGH2QJzc46P2

Obviously, this list isn't conclusive; you can always try others that are not in the list especially depending on where you decide to stay during your short stay in Rome. Also, where you eat will also depend on where you are within the city.

8

Nightlife

Even if Rome has for a long time been a religious city, this doesn't mean that there are no nice places to party. Therefore, I would suggest that you ensure that you are not overly exhausted during the day if you want to sample what Romans have to offer at night. Here are some popular night spots including bars & pubs, clubs and discos.

- **Goa Club**

This features a mix of local and international guest DJs that play house and techno tunes. It is quite lively!

Address:Via Giuseppe Libetta, 13, 00154 Roma
Phone:+39 06 574 8277
Goa Club Website
http://www.goaclub.com/
Goa Club Map
https://goo.gl/maps/2x8mgm4rVGL2

- **Freni e Frizioni**

This is a popular terrace that serves aperitivos and cocktails. It features elegant art and chandeliers.

Address:Via del Politeama, 4/6, 00153 Roma

Phone:+39 06 4549 7499
Freni e Frizioni Map
https://goo.gl/maps/ddt7WApWQgC2
· **Jonathan's Angels**

This is another popular bar and somewhat bizarre in various ways including its paintings, interior décor, toilets and the owner. It is interesting and has very friendly personnel; you will love it.

Address:Via della Fossa, 16, 00186 Roma
Jonathan's Angels Map
https://goo.gl/maps/o6TtqGJWc1K2

Tip: Piazza Navona and Via della Pace has many wine bars and cafes that you can try out if you happen to be within the area at night.

If you are a party animal, don't forget to go for a Colosseum Pub Crawl.
Note: dress for the party since party is always at its peak here.

Colosseum Pub Crawl Website
https://www.facebook.com/RomePubCrawl
Phone:+39 348 385 3432

Piazza Navona Map
https://goo.gl/maps/HCkQLZvHNJ72

Via della Pace Map
https://goo.gl/maps/vpfevoAY8aD2

Everything you have seen so far can be overwhelming; you might end up missing important places just because you don't have a plan of how you would tour Rome. Here is a sample 3 day itinerary for you to get started.

9

Hotels

Relais Palazzo Taverna

Relais Palazzo Taverna is a lovely hotel in a 12th-century build-ing.This hotel has an interesting style that is a combination between the 1960's style and modern, which creates something special.The hotel is located in an old part of Rome and has a nice warm atmosphere.

Address:Via Dei Gabrielli, 92, 00186 Roma
Phone:+39 06 2039 8064
Relais Palazzo Taverna Website
http://goo.gl/XsYY1u
Relais Palazzo Taverna Map
https://goo.gl/maps/heGii6e627J2

Palm Gallery Hotel

The Parm Gallery Hotel is located in a 1907 villa.The location is in one of Rome's upmarket suburbs and will take you about 30 minutes to central Rome.However, it is a lovely setting and well worth the travel.It is nice hideaway from the busy Rome streets.

Address:Via delle Alpi, 15, 00198 Roma
Phone:+39 06 6478 1859
Palm Gallery Hotel Website
http://goo.gl/eJAGPi
Palm Gallery Hotel Map
https://goo.gl/maps/FDTJmNzadzy

Suite Dreams Hotel

Suite Dreams Hotel is a modern minimalist hotel, so it's something different in comparison with the other hotels on this list.However, the hotel is lovely and has great service.The hotel has very affordable rates, free breakfast and comes with free WiFi and has most modern amenities.

Address:Via Modena, 5, 00184 Roma
Phone:+39 06 4891 3907
Suite Dreams Hotel Website
http://www.suitedreams.it/en/

Suite Dreams Hotel Map
https://goo.gl/maps/NeYbjhvF1vG2

Grand Hotel Gianicolo

Grand Hotel Gianicolo is probably one of the best and coolest places to stay in Rome.This palazzo is a fantastic traditional Italian design, and you will feel like you are in an old Italian movie.The hotel has fantastic service and has a big pool outside for you to take a swim.The location is a bonus.

Address:Viale delle Mura Gianicolensi, 107, 00152 Roma
Phone:+39 06 5833 3405
Grand Hotel Gianicolo Website
http://grandhotelgianicolo.it/en/
Grand Hotel Gianicolo Map
https://goo.gl/maps/2HWhDamxLXJ2

10

3 Day Itinerary

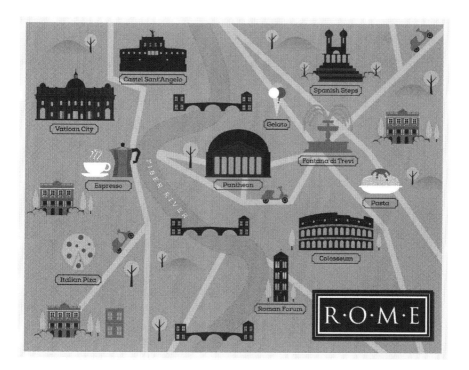

Day 1

Today you will visit everything between Palatine Hill and Spanish Steps. Here is how to go about it:

Start with the Roman Colosseum (buy a ticket at the Palatine hill ticket office to save on time you would otherwise waste in the queue).

Go up the Palatine Hill to have a panoramic view of Roman Forum and the central Rome then enter the Roman forum to explore it. Move on to the Capitoline Hill to find Piazza del Campidoglio and Capitoline Museums (just enjoy the view).

Take lunch bites around Piazza Venezia then marvel at Victor Emmanuel II monument while moving towards Piazza de la Rotonda. Move towards Pantheone then double back to the Trevi Fountain (you can take an ice cream here).

Make your way to the Borghese park to get a nice sun set view of the city. You can finally make your way towards the Trastevere to board a bus or metro or spend your evening in the nearby restaurants and bars.

Day 2

Today, you are going to visit the Vatican City to see everything including Sistine Chapel and Vatican Museum so it is best to wake up early to beat the line. You will probably get tired of seeing Michelangelo's ceiling after which you can move to the St. Peter's Basilica. Don't take too long though; move outside to the St. Peter's Square to admire the different statues around the area. If you are good at planning, it is even possible to meet the pope on Sundays and Wednesdays (if he is in town).

Take a lunch break at the nearby restaurants then move towards the old post office then take a stroll down the Tiber River where you will come across Castel 'Sant'Angelo or Vila Farnesina just near the Botanical gardens to get a feel of the famous Roman Renaissance.

You can now cross the river to explore the city's neighborhoods like Piazza Navona and Campo de Fiori (this is the flower market). This area is filled with bars and restaurants so you will be spoilt for choice on which to choose. If you want to party, it is time to dress up for a night of party. Alternatively, you can go for concerts, music and dance events to spend the night.

Day 3

Today, you will spend your morning exploring the Capitoline Museums; these three museums are connected by underground gallery so you will probably spend all your morning here exploring artifacts and artworks that tell of the ancient Roman world.

Take a lunch break along the Isola Tiberina. You can then spend the rest of your afternoon checking out what you didn't see well in the previous days. If you feel you already covered enough in day one and two, you can check out such places like The Baths of Diocletian at Piazza Repubblica and its Octagonal Hall.

You can also check out the Ancient Appian Way, which is just about 3km from the Colosseum. Be on the lookout for nature trails, catacombs, ruins and cafes along the way. If you love art, you might also want to check out the Borghese Gallery before your trip can come to an end. Nevertheless, you could also check out the Imperial Roman Forum in the evening or even visit the Colosseum at night just to marvel at its majesty and beauty.

Note:The ancient Rome has countless places to see that you definitely cannot exhaust in a 3 days visit so try to be reasonable with yourself because there is so much to cover within so little time.

11

Conclusion

I want to thank you for reading this book! I sincerely hope that you received value from it!

If you received value from this book, I want to ask you for a favour.Would you be kind enough to leave a review for this book on Amazon?

Check Out My other Books!!

https://www.amazon.com/Florence-Short-Travel-Italy-Guides-ebook/dp/B017L5ZNLW/